the ARMOR *of* GOD

Mark Fell

ISBN 978-1-64140-778-6 (paperback)
ISBN 978-1-64140-779-3 (digital)

Christian Faith Publishing, Inc.
832 Park Avenue
Meadville, PA 16335
www.christianfaithpublishing.com

Printed in the United States of America

PROLOGUE

The past twenty years of my life have been impacted by so many people who I have heard teach on the Armor of God or wrote books that I have been blessed to read. Although I cannot name everyone who impacted my life, I would like to say thank you. Thank you for sowing a seed that produced a desire in me to know more.

This book is a nine-week series that I preach every year for the sole purpose of equipping the body of Christ. I believe the body of Christ needs to have a good understanding about the Armor of God if they desire to live a victorious life. Just as I have gleaned nuggets over the past twenty years, my prayer is this book will not only help you learn more, but that it will also be a tool for you to use while helping others grow in their understanding.

God Bless,
Mark Fell

CHAPTER ONE

It Is Time to Stand

We live in a country that prides itself on its military. There is no doubt that we have the best military in the world. Every day, men and women get out of bed prepared to defend our country, and I thank God for them every day. They have been trained, prepared, and supplied with the provisions needed to accomplish the task set before them. We, as Christians, have also been given the provisions needed to win the battles in our lives.

You may be reading this book today, and you are one of the Christians who is facing a battle within your life. You know that the battle is spiritual, but it has taken its toll on you. Sometimes, you find yourself so beat down that you feel like giving up. Well, this is where the Armor of God comes in. It protects you in your battles, so you will not get wounded.

You see, without the full Armor of God being applied, you are vulnerable in certain areas of your life. These vulnerable areas are where the devil will attack because he can penetrate where there is no armor.

Everybody goes through battles. The difference is that some people apply the full armor of God every day, while others have not been trained to do so.

God has given us something to protect us, and we need to apply it to our lives while walking in it each day. It is time to quit depending on yourself and your own strength. Instead, start depending on God and in His strength.

We are sent to not only live a victorious life but to help a darkened, hell-bound, demon-ridden world along the way. We cannot do it within our own power.

It was, and still is, God's plan that His children have a supernatural ministry. It was, and still is, His plan for us to have power over the enemy! God's plan is for His supernatural power to destroy the work of the devil and to set men free. In order for that to come to pass, we have to put on the full Armor of God and not just part of it. So, within this book, I am going to explain how to apply the Armor of God piece by piece.

Ephesians 6:10 says, "Finally, my brethren, be strong in the Lord and in the power of His might."

Now the word finally in the Greek comes from the root word leipo which means to leave. Paul is saying" for the past five and a half chapters I have been telling you how to walk, how to talk, and how to live in the Lord, but if you want to be victorious leave that alone for a minute and pay close attention to what I am about to say because you can not walk, talk or live a victorious life in the Lord unless you have on the whole Armor of God. Success comes from the armor of God being applied to ones life because that is what protects us against the attacks of the enemy.

The phrase *Be Strong* in Ephesians 6:10 should be written *Be Made Strong* because there is a passive voice here that suggest that we cannot do it ourselves. It is in Jesus and his possession that we are made strong.

Now, the word strong means motion or action. We are to take an upright active position by being endued with energy/Gods sovering power. His might in this verse is His force and ability that works within believers for us to move forward.

We are to move forward by forgetting those things that are behind us. You are to leave your past victories in the past, because if you do not, you will be so wrapped up in them that you will never get another one.

In Matthew 17, there is a story of a boy that was demon-possessed. The disciples of Jesus tried to cast out the demon, but they could not. Now, in Matthew 10, Jesus had already sent them out to cast out demons, heal the sick, clean the lepers, and even raise the dead. But they could not cast out a demon from a child.

Matthew 17:19 (NKJV) says, "Then the disciples came to Jesus privately and said, "Why could we not cast it out?"

Verse 20 says, "So Jesus said to them, 'Because of your unbelief (because of doubt). For assuredly, I say unto you, if you have faith as a mustard seed, you will say to this mountain "move from here to there" and it will move and nothing will be impossible for you'."

Now watch this. Verse 21 says, "However, this kind of talking about faith does not go out except by prayer and fasting."

Go Out in the Greek means To Depart, Be Discharged, Proceed (Strong's Greek Lexicon, G1607).

It is not saying that you get faith by praying and fasting. Romans 10:17 says, "Faith comes by the Word of God." It is saying that faith is released in a greater capacity when you fast and pray, because fasting and praying gets you past your past and focuses you on your present and future. It moves you forward.

Not only are we to move on from our past victories, but especially from our past failures. If you do not, they will haunt you for the rest of your life. Listen, you cannot change your past because what is done is done, so move on and move forward into the blessings of God that he has for you now.

I like what Paul says in Philippians 3:12 (KJV). "Not that I have already attained or I am already perfected, but I press on that I may lay hold of that which Christ Jesus has also laid hold of me."

Philippians 3:13 (KJV) says, "Brethren, I do not count myself to have apprehended: but one thing I do, forgetting those things which are behind, and reaching forward to those which are ahead."

He forgot about the past so that he could move forward. We should use our past victories and past failures as a reference point. You see, a reference is something that brings consultation, or a source of information. We are not to live in it—neither good nor bad—but learn and reach forward.

That is what Paul is saying: *Be Strong,* move forward, and do not stop.

What are we to move forward in? Ephesians 6:10 (KJV) says," Be strong in the Lord, move forward in Jesus, and in his power." Which in Strong's Greek is *krat'-os* (G2904) and means dominion, might, power, and strength. *Of his might* means forcefulness or ability. The root word means to hold possession.

So, Paul is telling us that the way we move forward is in Jesus's power, His domain, and His authority. It is made available by His being connected with His possessions.

Where is His possessions? According to Ephesians 1:20–21 it is at "God's right hand in heavenly places. Far above all principalities and power and might and dominion and every name that is named, not only in this age but also in that which is to come."

If you are born again, bought, and washed by the precious blood of Jesus, then according to

Ephesians 2:6, you have been "made to sit tog
in heavenly places in Christ Jesus." The word ; ..wwe
means to give a seat in company with.

So, the seat has been prepared and given to us,
but it is our choice whether we sit in it or not. That
seat is a seat of authority that sits above cancer, heart
disease, diabetes, allergies, poverty, and everything
else that goes against the life that the Bible says we
can have as a child of God. If you are born again,
you were made to sit with Jesus in heavenly places
with authority!

"These signs shall follow those who believe: In
my name, they *(talking about the children of God
and talking about those who have taken their seat in
Christ Jesus)* will *(not might or even can)* cast out
devils. They will speak with new tongues; they will
take up serpents. If they drink anything deadly, it
will by no means hurt them. They will lay hands on
the sick, and they will recover" (Mark 16:17–18,
KJV). When will this happen for you? When you
realize who you are through Christ, these signs shall
follow.

In Luke 10:19 (KJV) Jesus says, "Behold, I give
you the power to tread on serpents, scorpions, and
over all the power of the enemy: and nothing shall
by any means hurt you." He is not just talking to

pastors and evangelists. He is talking to the whole body of born again believers.

It is God's desire that the whole body of Christ advance forward and invade the kingdom of darkness. It is not His desire to just take back, but take over. He is not talking about a select few doing this. He wants everybody to do it.

We are told in Romans 5:17 (NKJV), "For if by the one man's offense death reigned through the one, much more those who receive abundance of grace and of the gift of righteousness *will reign in life* through the one, Jesus Christ."

The word *reign* in the Greek means to rule. The root word tells us how. It is through a foundation of power and a sovereign king.

It is through Jesus that we have the right and the ability to reign in this life with the authority of a king. We are in a spiritual battle. Your family, friends, and loved ones who are hooked on drugs, pornography, or whatever ungodly thing that has them bound up are in a spiritual battle. You need to understand that there is a spirit behind that addiction, and it has a name. I've got good news. It has to bow to the name of Jesus!

Drug addiction has to bow to the name of Jesus. Alcoholism has to bow to the name of Jesus. Cancer has to bow to the name of Jesus. Diabetes has to bow to the name of Jesus. Lust has to bow to the name of Jesus. Luke warmness has to bow to the name of Jesus.

But to be able to enforce the authority that you have been given, you must put on the whole Armor of God.

Ephesians 6:11 (KJV) says, "Put on the whole (*not part*) Armor of God (*why?*) that ye may be able to stand against the wiles of the devil."

The word *stand* means an upright and active position.

The word *wiles* is where the English word *roads* comes from, and it means his methods that he uses; and according to verse 12, those methods are spiritual roads or avenues that he uses to invade our lives. Here is what God tells us to do about it.

Ephesians 6:13 says, "Wherefore, (*because of that*) taken unto you the *whole* Armor of God that ye may be *able* to withstand in the evil day and having done all to stand."

Because of the methods that the devil is going to use, put on the Armor of God and stand! He did not say that it would keep you out of the battle, but the Armor of God will protect you through the battle.

Here is something that we need to see. Four times within four verses, Paul tells us to take an upright and active position against the devil, but only after you have put on the whole Armor of God.

This is where some people get confused. They think that when they get saved, that the Armor of God is automatically applied in their life, but it is not. Paul tells us to put on the Armor of God. It is something that each individual has to apply to their own life.

The Armor that God has made for you is tailor-made for you. It is made to protect you through your battles because everyone's battles are not the same.

Take the story in 1 Samuel 17:38–39, for instance. David would not use Saul's armor for protection against his battle with Goliath because it did not fit him. You see, it was not made for him. It was made for Saul.

Paul tells us in Ephesians 6:11 to "put on the whole Armor of God." The phrase *put on* in the Greek means to sink down into a garment. Something that has been designed and made by God for you personally.

The Armor of God has been made available to you. Will you take the time to apply it?

In the next eight chapters, we are going to look at each piece of the Armor of God individually. We will be looking at what they are, what they protect, and how you apply them.

CHAPTER TWO

The Power to Withstand

I have been asked the question, "Why are you writing a book on the Armor of God?" My answer is that I am on a mission, and that mission is to give as many people as possible the understanding of what we are to do if we want to live a victorious life. I want every Christian to stand in the protection that has been provided for them by the Heavenly Father.

We all have the same adversary who "walks about like a roaring lion seeking whom he may devour" (1 Peter 5:8, NKJV) Without the Armor of God applied to our lives, we are easy prey.

We are in a spiritual battle, and the Armor of God is our spiritual warfare suit designed by God. It enables us to stand and win our spiritual battles that we face day to day.

God has given us everything we need to be protected and victorious, but it is up to us to apply it. In the words of Paul, "put on the whole Armor of God that you may be able to stand against the wiles of the devil" (Ephesians 6:11, NKJV)

Let us start with Ephesians 6:13 (NKJV). It says, "Therefore, take up the whole Armor of God that you may be able to withstand in the evil day and having done all to stand."

Paul is telling us that we cannot withstand the attacks of the enemy unless we have on the whole Armor of God.

The word *withstand* in Strong's Greek (G436) is *anti-histemi*, which means vigorously opposing, bravely resisting, and standing face to face against an adversary. In other words, standing your ground.

It is also where the English word *antihistamine* comes from. A histamine is what makes your sinuses go haywire. When you go to the doctor, they prescribe you an antihistamine, which puts a block on the histamine. This prevents them from messing up your sinuses.

Paul is telling us to withstand or "antihistamine up" with the authority and spiritual weapons that have been given to us as children of God. We need to begin fighting back and blocking the plots of the devil before they ever take hold.

Doctors prescribe certain antihistamines to be taken daily. This not only gets rid of the sinus problems that we may already have, but also prevents new ones from forming.

You are going to go through some battles in your life, but some of them can be avoided or made less devastating by simply withstanding them. In order to be able to withstand, you must have on the whole Armor of God.

When you read and take Ephesians 6:10–20 in the context that Paul wrote it in, you will understand that a child of God who has on the whole Armor of God is able to defeat the devil every single time. I do not know about you, but to me, that is shouting grounds!

Paul said in Ephesian's 6:13 (NKJV) that you may be able to withstand in the evil day. You are able to vigorously oppose, bravely resistant, and stand face to face against your advisory while standing your ground.

A good example is Shammah in 2 Samuel 23:11–12 (NKJV). Verse 11 says, "And after him was Shammah, the son of Agee the Hararite. The Philistines had gathered together into a troop where there was a piece of ground full of lentils. So the people fled from the Philistines." Verse 12 says, "But he stationed himself in the middle of the field, defending it, and killed the Philistines. So the Lord brought about a great victory."

Shammah understood that if he ran, the field would be lost. He made the decision that enough was enough, and he placed himself in a position to fight for what belongs to him. Because of his stand, God brought a victory in his life.

That is what the Armor of God does. It gives you the offensive and defensive weapons that you need to be victorious in life.

Have you ever heard someone say that they do not feel saved? We should have a "know-so" salvation, and the knowledge of salvation comes by having on the whole Armor of God.

Another misconception about the Armor of God is that people say that we are to apply it every day. Wrong! We are never told to take it off once we have applied it. If you take it off even for a minute, you are defenseless against the attacks of the enemy. We are to strengthen our armor every day, but never take it off.

After a battle, the Roman soldiers would go to the blacksmith to have their armor repaired, but they would not leave the blacksmith's shop without it. It was their protection. We are supposed to repair our armor—and strengthen our armor—by spending time in the Word of God, praying, fasting, and getting into His presence. Never go to battle with messed-up armor because every crack and dent is a weak spot. When you come out of a battle, spend as much time as you possibly can in the Word of God and His presence, so you will be prepared to face the next battle.

Listen, you are going to go through battles in your life whether you are prepared or not. We have one adversary, and that is the devil. He is walking around like a roaring lion just waiting to devour you. He is looking to see where you are standing with God and looking to see where your faith is at.

The devil is compared to a lion. If you know anything about lions, you know that they sneak up on their prey when they least expect it, when they let their guard down, and when they are at rest. They do not attack a herd. They find the ones who have strayed off by themselves. When the time is right, they attack.

In Hebrews 10:25 (NKJV) it says, "Not forsaking the assembling together of ourselves as in the manner of some, but exhorting one another, and so much take more as you see the day approaching."

The writer of Hebrews is telling us that we need church. We need to hear the preaching of the gospel. We need the fellowship. We need the accountability even more than our forefathers did.

Make the extra effort. Make it your priority to be in church. You should not only be in church, but you should also be active in church. Let the iron sharpen iron. When the battle does come, you will be prepared, ready to station yourself, and fight the good fight of faith. God can bring about a great victory in your life this way.

CHAPTER THREE

The Loin Belt

The first piece of the armor we come to is the Loin Belt of Truth.

Ephesians 6:14 in the Amplified Bible says, "Stand; Therefore, [hold your ground], having tightened the belt of truth around your loins."

In everyday life, most people do not pay attention to what kind of belt people wear, whether it is big, little, black, or brown. It is just one of those things that do not normally cross our minds. Yet, it was the first piece of the armor Paul mentioned.

The loin belt was possibly the most important piece of the armor that the soldier had. It is what held the armor together. Let us face it. Although some belts are decorated and used as fashion statements, the main use is to keep your pants in place.

If our pants are too big, we put on a belt to tighten it up and solve the problem.

If a soldier did not wear his loin belt and have it in place for some reason, then the rest of his armor would not stay in place either. It helped hold up his shield, it held his sword, and it held his dagger. Without his loin belt on, he would not be very effective. Not only that, it also took some of the weight of his breastplate off of his shoulders while supporting his lower back.

Our loin belt is the Loin Belt of Truth, which is the Word of God. It is the most important weapon we have because the rest of our weapons will not work without it.

Just as the soldier had to wear his loin belt to keep his armor together, we must put on the Loin Belt of Truth if we want to walk in the Armor of God.

The Bible says in Proverbs 4:20-22 (KJV), "My son, attend to my words; incline your ear to my sayings. Do not let them depart from your eyes; keep them in the midst of your heart. For they are life to those who find them, and health to all their flesh.

The Amplified Bible says in verse 22, "For they (*talking about the Word of God*) are life to those who find them, and healing and health to all their flesh."

The words *life* in Strong's Hebrew is *chay* (H2416). It means alive, fresh, and maintenance. The root word that *chay* comes from its root *chayah* (H2421). It means to live, to receive, to give life, to nourish, to preserve, and to quicken.

The Word of God does not only bring life, but it also maintains life by giving nourishment. The Word of God has to be the foundation on which you build your Christian walk.

How do we know that you can be saved? The Word of God tells us that we can. How do we know that we can be filled with the Holy Ghost? The Word of God tells us that we can. How do we know that we have a right standing with God through Jesus? How do we know that we can have joy? How do we know that we can have a prosperous life? The Word of God tells us. It is the Word of God that tells us who we are, what we have, and what we can accomplish as Christians of God.

Here is a question for the times. How do you increase your faith? You may be surprised, but according to Romans 10:17, "Faith comes by hearing and hearing comes by the Word of God." So, the only way your faith grows is by continually hearing the Word of God.

The loin belt is a natural piece of weaponry. It holds the offensive and defensive weapons. So, what is this telling us? It is telling us that the Word of God will keep us balanced. It is what keeps us from being "tossed to and fro and carried about with every wind of doctrine." (Ephesians 4:14, KJV) It is important that we have a firm foundation to stand on.

We are told in James 1:21 (NKJV), "Therefore, lay aside all filthiness and overflow of wickedness and receive with meekness the implanted word, which is able to save your souls." Now, your soul is your mind, your will, and your emotions—or the natural drive of the flesh. If left unchecked, it will get caught up in filthiness and wickedness.

James tells us to combat that by implanting the Word of God in us. The Greek word for *implanted* is *emphutos* (G1721). It draws its root meaning from *En* (G1722), which means to germinate, to grow, or to spring up and produce.

We are being told that we are changed when we sow the seed of the gospel into our lives. When that seed is sown, it then begins to germinate, or grow, changing our very nature to imitate God. Read Ephesians 5:1.

This is why Paul focused on the loin belt first. Not only was it the soldiers most important part of the armor, giving them the support to carry the rest of their armor. To us, it is also the foundation that gives us the ability to carry and use the weapons that have been given to us.

One last part of the loin belt that I want to talk about is the buckle. Because without the buckle to hold it together, it would be a loin strap. It is a belt, so what is the buckle?

We know the loin belt is the Word of God. So the buckle is what holds it all together, and that is salvation. The buckle is:

1) believing that Jesus is the son of God;
2) believing He lived a perfect sinless life;
3) believing that he chose to die in our place on the cross to be buried in a borrowed tomb;
4) believing that he arose from the dead three days later;
5) believing that he now sits at the right hand of God making intercession for us.

Your whole Christian walk hangs on you believing this. When you believe this, and accept Jesus as the Lord and Savior, you get into the Word of God. God then wraps the truths of His Word around you, and it supports your every moment. He gives you the ability to apply the rest of the armor, so that you can live a victorious life. This is what the loin belt does in your life.

CHAPTER FOUR

Breast Plate of Righteousness

In the previous chapter, we learned about the Loin Belt of Truth, which is the most important piece of the Armor of God. The rest of the armor relies on your belt being in place. It holds your offensive and defensive weapons. Paul put the belt first because you cannot get any other piece of the armor unless you first have on the Loin Belt of Truth. The Word of God is the base to apply all other pieces to your life.

Once you take that step, commit your life to Christ, and begin to study the Word of God, the Breast Plate of Righteousness is waiting on you.

Now, when Paul was describing the Armor of God to the church at Ephesus, he was relating it to the Roman soldier's armor of their time.

Now, the breast plate was the shiniest and most glamorous piece of weaponry that the Roman soldier had in his possession. It covered from the bottom of his chin all the way down to the top of his knees.

It was made up of two pieces. One covered the front while the other covered the back. They used either bronze or brass for the material. They would cut the metal into small pieces, similar to the scales on a fish, and then fasten them together so they overlapped one another. As the soldier wore his breast plate and walked around with it on, these small pieces would rub together and become more reflective with each step. In the sunlight, the breast plate would give off a rainbow color effect. When the whole army walked together, it would be so bright that it would temporarily blind the enemy. That is why the Roman soldiers chose to fight facing the sun. It gave them an extra advantage. Logic tells us that if we are fighting an enemy that is blinded, then it is easier to gain the victory.

After the Philistines cut Samson's hair, they also poked out his eyes. They knew that in time, his hair would grow back. If his strength came back with his hair, at least he would not be able to see them and use his strength against them. This was the mindset of the Roman soldiers. You cannot defeat what you cannot see.

Just as the breast plate was designed to be a defensive weapon to protect them from the blows of the enemy, so is the Breast Plate of Righteousness.

Your adversary, the devil, wants to make you think that you are not righteous. He wants you to think that you are a nobody, and God can never use anyone who has done what you have done. He wants you to think that you are unworthy.

Here is what the Bible says in 2 Corinthians 5:21, KJV: "For He hath made Him to be sin for us, who knew no sin; that WE might be made the righteousness of God in Him.""

Jesus became the ultimate sin offering for us. "So that in and through Him we might become (*endued with, viewed as being in, and examples of*) the righteousness of God (*what we ought to be, approved and acceptable, and in the right relationship with him by His goodness*) (2 Corinthians 2:21, AMP)

Righteousness means right standing. How do we obtain the right standing? Romans 10:10 says, "For with the heart man believeth unto righteousness and with the mouth confession is made unto salvation."

We obtain a right standing with God not based on our past, or what we have done or not done. It is based on us accepting the work done at the cross. Our life does not make us right with God. Accepting the life that comes through Jesus is what makes us right with God.

We have to learn to walk in the righteousness of God. It is one of our weapons of defense against all the slanderous accusations and outrageous strategies of the devil. In order to be able to do that, you have got to believe in your righteousness; and the only way that is going to happen is if you walk in the spirit and not your flesh.

You see the word *heart* in Romans 10:10 means your thoughts or *feelings*. The word *salvation* means *deliver* and *health*.

Now, the Bible tells us in Luke 6:45, "For out of the abundance of the heart the moth speaks." In Mark 11:23, "He will have whatever he says."

This is telling us you will have or become what you speak. You will speak what you believe. In other words, confession of our beliefs makes them a reality in our lives. You will have what you say, and you will say what you believe.

It is time that we quit believing what the devil says about us and what people say about us. It is time to start believing what the Word of God says about us.

If you are saved, then you have been "made the righteousness of God in Him. (Jesus)" (2 Corinthians 5:21).

It has been said that there are over 3,000 promises in the Word of God for the children of God. We need to learn every one of them, so we can use them against the devil's lies.

The reason being as we walk in the righteousness of God, we will become more beautiful and more blinding to the eyes of the enemy—just as the Roman soldier's breast plate would become more beautiful and blinding with each and every step. Not only that, we also become a light to a darkened world.

Matthew 5:14–16 (KJV) says, "Ye are (*not should be but are*) the light of the world. A city that is set on a hill cannot be hidden. Neither do men light a candle and put it under a bushel. But on a candlestick; and it giveth light unto all that are in the house. Let *your* light so shine before men that they may see *your* Father which is in heaven."

We are light in the midst of darkness. As the old saying goes, we should stick out like a sore thumb. We are not to hide ourselves in the midst of the world that we live in. We are to be seen. If we are walking and living like we are supposed to be, then we cannot be hidden.

It is by the works God does through us that bring Him the glory. So, how dare we say, "I am humbling myself by hiding what God is doing in my life"." That is not humbling our self. That is keeping Him from receiving the glory. The reason people do this is because they have been lied to about who they are. If you are saved, then you are light. You are a beacon. You are a child of God. You are the righteousness of God in Christ Jesus.

You need to go ahead and accept it. You are not who you were. You are not an old sinner saved by grace. You are a child of God who has been saved by grace. That is what the Word of God calls you. That is how God sees you. He does not see you as a sinner. He sees you as His child and His beloved. So why do people want to claim to be a sinner saved by grace? They do not know who they are. You may have messed up, and you may mess up again. If you repent, you are saved which means you are a child of God. Prove it. Okay?

Romans 8:14 (KJV) says, "For as many are led by the spirit of God, these are sons of God."

Romans 8:16–17 (NKJV) says, "The spirit himself bears witness with our spirit that we are children of God, and if children, then heirs. Heirs with God and joint heirs with Christ."

2 Corinthians 5:17 says, "Therefore if anyone is in Christ, he is a new creation (*renovated*). The old things has passed away (*what you were is gone*) behold *all* things are new."

When you get saved, God renovates you. He tears out all of the old stuff that is no good and replaces it with new, fresh, and up-to-date materials. These materials have not been scarred or messed up. On the outside, you may still look the same. On the inside, you are new again!

Then it goes on to say in 2 Corinthians 5:21 (NKJV), "For He made Him who knew no sin to be sin for us, that we might become the righteousness of God in him."

Did you read that? But what is righteousness? We know it means right standing with God, but what does that really mean? The word *righteousness* means justification (equality: the amount that a property is worth beyond what is owed on it). It also means innocent while the root word means to show.

Jesus paid the full value price for you, and now he wants to show you off to the world. The price that Jesus paid was for everyone that will receive it as 2 Corinthians 5:17 states. Now, we need to see the full accomplishment of the price that Jesus paid. Righteousness deals with the amount that a property is worth not what is owed on it. Let me explain. If Jesus would have just paid the price owed for humanity, then only those who were alive then and in that part of the world could have been saved.

But He went beyond what was owed at the time and paid the full value price for all humanity. Romans 10:13 (NKJV) states, "whoever calls upon the name of the Lord shall be saved." Regardless of what they have done, they are only one decision of repentance away from salvation. The reason that He paid the full value price is so "That we might become the righteousness of God in him."

So how do we become righteous? How do we apply the breast plate of righteousness? The first step is that you must be saved. The second step is that you must study the Word of God and see that you have the right to stand before God because of what Jesus did. Do not stop there. You need to confess who you are and what you have rights to because of what Jesus did.

Because of Jesus, I am righteous! I am justified! I am innocent! I have a right standing with God! I am not who I used to be! I am a born-again child of the one and only true living God! The creator of the universe! I call him Father and He calls me child! That is a reason to shout. I have been renovated!

So, when the devil comes to you and tells you that you will not amount to anything, that you are worthless, and that God will not hear you, you need to stand to your feet, poke your chest out, and very boldly tell him, "I am the righteousness of God in Christ Jesus! I have a right standing with god because I have accepted Jesus as my Lord and Savior! I am somebody, and I am a child of God! God always hears my prayers because the greater one lives on the inside of me. So, devil, you lose again!"

This assurance comes by being a child of God, standing on his word, and obeying what he says. So, the Breast Plate of Righteousness is applied by knowing your rightful place as a child of God. Knowing that because Jesus is your Lord and Savior, you have now been justified to stand in communion with God.

Now, I do not know about you, but I think this is something worth shouting about! Knowing that I can come before the creator of the universe whenever I need to—or whenever I want to. I can call him Father and have Him answer.

Take a moment and ask yourself these questions. Am I saved? If I died right now, do I know for sure that I would go to heaven? If you said no, or if you say you are not sure, but right now you want that assurance that your name is written in the Lambs book of Life, keep reading. In order to do that, the Bible says in Romans 10:9 (NKJV), "That if you confess with your mouth the Lord Jesus and believe in your heart that God has raised him from the dead. You will be saved." Verse 10 (NKJV) says, "For with the heart one believes unto righteousness, and with the mouth confession is made unto salvation." Verse 13 (NKJV) says, "For whoever calls on the name of the Lord shall be saved."

Jesus, forgive me. Renovate me. Make me new again. Right now, I accept you as my Lord and Savior. My life has been bought with the price that was paid at Calvary, and now I am a child of God. I have a right standing with God, and from this day forward, I will live and be a blessing to my Father in Heaven. In Jesus name, Amen.

CHAPTER FIVE

Shoes of Peace

The purpose of this book is to help prepare you for what God wants to do in you, for you, and through you. It is also supposed to help you take a stand. In order to stand, you must have on the whole Armor of God. There will be people who you come in contact with that will talk about you, lie about you, and try to tear you down. You need to realize that these people are nothing more than what I call barking dogs. I have learned that a barking dog does not bite. It is the ones who growl that will take a bite out of you. The main reason those people talk about you is because they are jealous and sometimes scared of what God is doing in your life. Do not pay attention to their barks and stay focused on the journey that God has set before you. We serve a miraculous God who desires to do miraculous things for those whose heart is stayed upon him.

Ephesians 6:15 (KJV) says, "And your feet shod with a preparation of the gospel of peace."

The word *shod* Strong's Greek (G5265) means to bind under ones feet. This means to put on shoes, or sandals, and bind them on your feet.

The Romans' shoes were made up of two pieces. One covered the lower legs, and the other part was the shoe itself. The leg armor was called the graves. It was made up of a hard metal because if the enemy could get close enough, he would try to kick him in the shin to break their shin bone and cause them to fall down. If you are lying on your back on the ground in the middle of war, you are as good as dead. There are a lot of Christians lying on their backs on the ground in the spirit because they have not shod their feet with the gospel. What happened was the enemy came rushing in, broke their spiritual shin bone, and they fell to the ground—all because they did not know what is written in the Word of God. Let me explain what the shin guard is. The shin guard is the written word of God and you use it by telling the devil what is written in the word of God such as "Devil by the stripes that Jesus bore I am healed".

What about the shoes? We are told to have our feet shod. We are to have something bound on our feet, and that something is preparation of the gospel of peace. The word *preparation* Strong's Greek (G2091) means basis, foundation, firm footing. Ephesians 6:15 is the only place in the New Testament where the word occurs in relation to the use of the military shoe.

Paul is telling us that if we want to be able to stand against the attacks of the devil, then we must have a firm footing or foundation of the gospel in our lives. It is a firm and solid knowledge of the gospel in the believer's life that will make their stand in God firm and unmovable in the midst of an attack.

When Paul was preaching this, the people had a visual picture of the shoes worn by the Roman soldiers of that time. Their shoes were not ordinary shoes. The soldiers were furnished with shoes that had one inch to three-inch hobnails covering their sole. Hobnails were steel spikes that were used to grip the ground in a fight. They gave the soldiers the edge needed to win. They used them like a football player would wear cleats. They planted them in the ground to give them the foundation needed to push the enemy to the ground. When they got the enemy on the ground, they would use the hobnails to stomp them to death. The Word of God gives us the edge to win every battle in our lives.

When these soldiers walked down the cobblestone roads in Rome, it struck fear into the people around. You could hear them coming from miles away, and as soon as the people heard them coming, they would get out of the way because those Roman soldiers would not stop for anyone. If you got in the way, they would knock you down and keep on marching.

I tell people, "Do not get in my way because I am not slowing down much less stopping for anyone. I have been commissioned by my heavenly father to do a job, and I am determined to see it finished. If you want to go with me, fall in line and start marching." He said to preach the gospel, lead the lost to Christ, prepare my people for battle, and teach them how to walk in victory. In order to walk in victory, you must have on the whole Armor of God.

The Roman soldiers understood the necessity of always being prepared to fight. Every morning, they would apply their shoes to their feet. They knew the importance, and they knew how to use them.

What about you? Are you marching over your enemies? Or are you stopping for them? Are you one who is stopping because someone said it cannot be done? Because someone said God does not want to move in your life like that? They say those kinds of blessings are for the chosen few.

Well, the Word of God tells us in Acts 10:34 (KJV), "Then Peter opened his mouth and said, "'In the truth I perceive that God shows not partiality'""; or Romans 2:11 says, "For there is no partiality with God." The word *partiality* (Strong's Greek, G4382) in the Greek means favoritism or respect of persons. If he will do it for one, then he will do it for everyone.

Our text says and your feet shod with the preparation of peace. The word *peace* (Strong's Greek, G1515) means the implementing of health, welfare, prosperity, every kind of good into every aspect of one's life. The broad definition is the gospel, which leads to bliss.

It is not a onetime thing—it is something that can be achieved continually as you study the Word of God.

Every day, the Roman soldiers would sharpen their hobnails on the sandals just in case a surprise attack happened.

Let me ask you a question. Why did you go to class every day while you were in school? It was to prepare. What did you have to prepare for? Scheduled tests were not that bad, but those pop tests would cause you to fail if you had not prepared beforehand. We had a lot of them when I was in school.

It is the same way with your Christian walk. God urges us in 2 Timothy 2:15 to study the Word of God, because your adversary is not going to call you on the phone and ask you if it is okay if he brings a test, or trial your way next Thursday about 3:45 p.m. He is just going to show up, and you better be ready.

God has good things prepared for you, but the devil wants to tear you down. He does not want you to be prepared, so he is not going to check with you first to see if you are ready. He will just show up.

So many lessons can be learned from the lives of Shadrach, Meshach, Abednego, and Daniel. They had on their Gospel shoes. They were prepared when faced with adversity.

They did not have to weigh out the situation or circumstances first to see if it was worth it. They said, "We are not going to bow down." Or, in Daniel's, case, "I am not going to quit praying." Whatever you decide, my God has got this. Rather it is through the fire or through the lion's den, My

God has got it! They had full trust in God and His ability to deliver them.

In school, my daughter was a flyer on the cheerleading team. She could have had the best base in the world, but if she had not trusted them, it would have done her no good. Just like she had to trust her base to catch her, you have to trust that God has got you.

Let me explain this one more time. The word *shod* means to bind on one's feet. The words *preparation* and *gospel* is the phrasing meaning to be fit and prepared. The word *peace* means complete prosperity in every aspect of your life.

This is what the Word of God does. It will prepare you and cause you to prosper in every area of your life. That includes your health, finances, favor, and spiritual walk. It will keep you from falling away from Christ just because someone hurt you.

Your spiritual shoes look like the Romans' physical shoes, and here is how you use them. Has God ever told you to stand on a certain scripture? Does the devil come along and tell you, "It will not work"; "You are going to fall."; "That is not what that scripture means."; "That scripture is not for those of today, just those who lived when Jesus walked the earth."

When you have the peace on the bottom of your feet, when you know that the Word of God is true, that it means what it says, you cannot be moved! Not by what you see, not by what you hear, not by what you feel.

Listen, this is not you, but rather God using His peace and your feet. So, when the devil comes along and tells you that you are going to die with cancer, all you have to do is slam your foot down on his head and say, "No way, devil!" For it is written, "by His (*Jesus*) Stripes I am healed" (1 Peter 2:24, NKJV)!

When the devil tells you that you are a nobody, slam your foot on his head and declare, "Oh, yes, I am someone, devil, for it is written. "The spirit himself bears witness with our (*my*) spirit that we (*I*) are children of God" (Romans 8:16, ESV)!

When the devil comes and tells you that you're always going to be broke, slam your foot on the ground and tell him, "No! I am not devil!" For it is written, "God has given me the power to get wealth" (Deuteronomy 8:18).

It does not matter how I feel! It does not matter what my bank account looks like! It does not matter what the devil says about me because I have insight on the matter.

I have my hobnails dug down deep into the Word of God. I am not going to be moved by what I see; I am not going to be moved by what I hear; and I am not going to be moved by what I feel. I am moved by the Word of God and only the Word of God.

You see, I have got my foot on the rock and my mind is made up.

There will be times when the devil will stand in front of you and try to oppose both you and God.

Do not stop to ask him to move, just keep marching. Just keep on stomping, and just keep on pounding as you move forward in God's plan for your life. Be sure to do as much damage as you possibly can to him—he deserves it.

I, not only as a pastor but as a child of God, am tired of seeing mountains stopping children of God from getting the blessings that, not only God has for them, but rightfully belongs to them. It is time to tell that mountain to get out of your way.

I have got some good news. Are you ready? God wants to bless you more than you are being blessed.

So, with all of that, it brings up the question. How do you apply the Shoes of Peace? You apply the Shoes of Peace by telling the devil it is written, and then stand on that which is written without backing down. You apply the Shoes of Peace by holding first the promises of God and speaking them out of your mouth. You apply the Shoes of Peace by standing firm on the Word of God and putting into action that which you have learned.

I believe a lot of Christians need to start reading the Bible from the Table of Contents and not stop until they hit the maps. Go on and read the maps too.

Jesus won the battle for us! Victory is ours! Do you realize that you not only get the victory, but along with victory, the spoils that accompany it?

In 2 Chronicles chapter 20, it talks about a vast army coming against Jehoshaphat. As they began to sing and praise God, he set ambushes against the army who was invading Judah, and the armies were defeated. So, Jehoshaphat and his men went to carry off their plunder, and they found among them a great amount of equipment, clothing, and articles of value—more than they could ever carry at one time. There was so much plunder that it took three days to collect it!

And it says that when they got back to Jerusalem and entered, they went to the temple and worshipped God. The Bible says in 2 Chronicles 20:29, "The fear of God came on all kingdoms when they heard how the Lord had fought against the enemies of Israel and the kingdom of Jehoshaphat was at peace for his God had given him rest on every side."

It is time the children of God get what belongs to them! The knowledge of what belongs to you comes through the knowledge of God's word.

The Word of God will work if you work it. We work it by believing it, and speaking it out of our mouth as we obey it.

Just as the Roman shoes could be heard and struck fear into their enemies lives, it also strikes fear into the devil when you speak the Word of God out of your mouth by faith, because he knows the Word of God will defeat him every time it is used in faith.

CHAPTER SIX

Shield of Faith

Let me start out with an eye opening statement: "If you are living a defeated life it is because you choose to, not because you have to.

It is not Gods plan for you to live a defeated life. He wants you living a *victorious* life and He has made available everything that you need in order to live that victorious life—but it is up to you to receive the tools that He has provided and use them.

The word says in Ephesians 6:16 (NKJV), "Above all taking the shield of faith with which you will be able to quench the fiery darts of the wicked one."

The word *above* translates to superimposition which means to put on top of something else.

The word *all* means the whole, and the word *taking* means to get ahold of.

Paul is telling us to get ahold of the shield of faith because without it, you will not be victorious against the devil. So, with that in mind let us take a look at the shield.

First of all, the shield was always inseparably linked to the soldier's loin belt—just like our faith is linked to our loin belt of truth, the Word of God. If you do not give Gods word proper place in your life and continually study it, it will be only a matter of time before the faith that you have begins to dwindle and eventually dies. That's why you must not neglect the word.

The Roman soldier had three different shields. The first one was for public parades and ceremonies. It was small. It was pretty, but useless in battle because it was made of a thin metal. If you got close enough, you could take a small sword or knife and stick it through that shield because it was only for decoration and show.

Unfortunately, that is what a lot of Christians use. They hear something preached but refuse to study it out for themselves—therefore, it will not grow and produce a strong lasting faith.

They will say "My faith is strong because I heard so and so preach on this certain subject and my answer is "Well I am glad that they preached on that 'they got the revelation but understand you cannot obtain something from someone else's faith and revelation you have to have your on faith and revelation on the subject and your faith is established by you studying the word of God for yourself.

The second shield was a small forearm shield. It was used for hand-to-hand combat. The problem with this shield was, as long as you were fighting one person, you would be good and protected. But in war you may start out one-on-one, and it won't be long before you are outnumbered. So, Paul skipped this shield and went straight to the third one, called the war shield. An interesting fact is the same word for this shield is where our English word *door* comes from.

This shield was shaped like a door. It was around four-and-a-half foot wide. It was not anything fancy, but it was big enough to squat behind and be completely covered.

Romans 12:3 says, "God has dealt everyone of us a measure of faith." That measure is enough to make sure we are completely covered from head to toe, from inside out.

The problem is, most of the time, people will not take up their faith, or they haven't taken care of it. They haven't nourished it with the spirit and the Word of God. They have let it dry rot.

God does not give one person more faith then He does another. We were all given the same measure. But what you do with the faith that you were given determines how fast your faith grows, or if it grows at all.

If you don't nourish it with the spirit and the Word of God it will dry rot.

The Shield that Paul was referring to was made up of two layers of laminated wood, covered first with linen, and then with six layers of animal hide that was woven together, and then bound top to bottom with iron.

We are talking about something that is tough and durable, but it required oiling everyday so that it would not crack under pressure, or fall apart. That is why they cannot find a lot of war shields—dead men don't oil shields. So, the shields fell apart and disintegrated.

That's the same way with our faith. It requires daily anointing of the Holy Ghost, and strengthening of the Word of God so that we won't crack or fall apart under pressure.

We cannot live on past experiences with God. We need an everyday experience to grow, develop, and to keep our faith alive and active.

In Luke 9:37–42, a man brought his demon possessed child to the disciples to cast out the spirit, but they couldn't. It was not because they didn't have the authority, but rather because they didn't have the faith.

In Luke 9:1, Jesus gave them power and authority over all demons and diseases. When you study this, they operated in that power and authority to the point that they rejoiced about it—but now, they could not cast out a spirit and Jesus said that they were faithless. The center margin notes in the Bible says *unbelieving*.

You see, faith is not in the past, like memories. Hebrews 11:1 says faith is Now, in the present.

You can't live and operate off past experiences, or stale faith. In 2 Thessalonians 1:3 (KJV), it says, "we are bound to thank God always for you bretheren, as it is meet, because that your *faith growth exceedingly*."

So, your faith can grow. It can be either strong or weak, developed or undeveloped.

Past experiences are good to remember, but current faith has to come from a current revelation of our authority in God.

So, it's up to us on what kind of faith we have— weak, strong, developed, or undeveloped.

Jude 20 (KJV) tells us, ""But ye beloved building up yourself on your most holy faith praying in the Holy Ghost"."

The phrase ""*building up* can be translated to charging—like you would charge a battery.

So, we know faith comes from understanding the word through Romans 10:17. And according to Jude 20, that faith is charged by praying in the Holy Ghost, which produces the current faith that's active and alive that Heb. 11:1 speaks about.

One statement, that has been credited to Charles Finney, says, ""All prayer and no word you will blow up, All word and no prayer and you will dry up, but the word mixed with prayer and you will grow up."" So true.

The other thing about the soldiers' shield was that it had to be saturated in water, so that it could extinguish the fiery arrows of the enemy.

The enemies would use arrows set on fire, while carrying packs of oil and other liquids that would burst into flames upon impact. So, the soldiers were able to use their water-soaked shields to extinguish the arrows before they could do any damage.

Ephesians 5:26 says, "We are washed by the water of the word."

F.F. Bosworth, in his book Christ the Healer, said, ""Most Christians feed their body three hot meals a day, and their spirit one cold snack a week, and they wonder why they are so weak in faith"?"

Romans 10:17 (NKJV) says, "Faith comes by hearing and hearing by the Word of God."

The word ""*hearing* can be translated to mean *understanding*. It is when you actively understand the Word of God that your faith begins to grow. So, your faith is strengthened by feeding on the Word of God and then exercising it—but you must start where you are at.

You see, everybody started out with the same amount of faith. Some people have just been fed and exercised theirs more than others. If you're not to the place to where you can believe God to heal a headache, than you will not be able to raise the dead yet—and to get to that place, we must have active faith.

Our faith is activated when we study the Word of God and pray in the spirit. So, when the enemy comes at us, we are ready for him; our shields are prepared for battle.

But what happens if a whole cohort attacks us at one time? The Bible says one can put a thousand to flight, but two can put ten thousand to flight. When the Roman army was threatened by a mass opposition, the soldiers would walk very close to one another in a long line, side by side. Their shields had hinges on the sides of them, and they would fasten them together to form a massive wall of protection that allowed them to march right up to their enemy.

The Bible says in James 5:14 (KJV), "Is any sick among you? Let him call for the elders of the church; and let them pray over him, anointing him with oil in the name of the Lord."

Matthew 18:19 (KJV) says, "Again I say unto you, that if two of you shall agree on earth as touching anything that they shall ask it shall be done for them of my Father which is heaven."

When I have a problem that seems big, I just hook my faith up with someone who has similar faith, because if I can take care of a thousand, two can take care of ten thousand, three can take care of a hundred thousand, four can take care of a million, and so on—you get the idea.

But in the same way, if I have a problem and I go to someone who doesn't believe in healing, prosperity—or whatever I may stand in need of—and I hook up with their faith, it will not increase the action of faith. But rather it will decrease the action of faith.

One faith plus one faith equals ten thousand; then one faith plus one negative faith will equal a hundred. It will decrease at the same percentage as it increases. It will decrease your chances of victory, if you go to someone who cannot believe for what you need.

So, find someone with the like-minded faith and hook shields with them, and command the devil to return what he has stolen from you. Give back lost loved ones, give back health, give back finances, give back blessings, or whatever it may be that he has stolen. They belong to the children of God, so take them back and use them to glorify God.

There is power in faith and there is power in unity. The two combined are deadly forces against the kingdom of darkness. We are not called to sit back and do nothing. We are called to take over. So, let's prepare and use our shields of faith, and walk in the victory that Jesus paid for us to walk in.

CHAPTER SEVEN

Helmet of Salvation

Ephesians 6:17 says, "Take the helmet of salvation."

The soldier's helmet was very ornate. It looked more like a piece of art than a helmet of war. It was decorated with all kinds of engravings and etchings. On top was a plume line of bright colors made of feathers and horse hair.

The helmet was usually made of bronze and designed specifically to protect the cheeks and jaws. It was heavy, so they would fill the inside with sponge to make it more comfortable for the soldier to wear.

The helmet was very hard to pierce and the soldier would wear it at all times because their enemies carried a short-handled battle axe. If they did not have their helmet on, they would literally lose their head.

Now, our salvation is the most beautiful, wonderful gift that God ever gave us—but that is not what we are talking about here. Paul is talking to Christians here. What he is talking about is putting on knowledge of our salvation—about what is entitled to us because we are born-again children of God.

Salvation is what God does in your life when you repent and receive Jesus as Lord and savior of your life. But we are to put on the helmet of salvation by studying the Word of God.

> 2 Timothy 2:15 (KJV) says, "study to show thyself approved unto God, a workman that needeth not to be ashamed, rightly dividing the word of truth."

2 Timothy 3:16–17 (KJV) says, "All scripture is given by inspiration of God, and is profitable for doctorine, for reproof, for correction, for instruction in righteousness: that the man of God may be perfect thoroughly furnished unto all good works."

So, this is something that we have to do by studying the Word of God. And the reason is because the Bible says in 1 Peter 5:8 (KJV), "Be strong, be vigilant; because your adversary the devil, as roaring lion, walketh about, seeking whom he may devour."

The word *devour* in that verse means to take into one's mind; the word *picture* would be to scramble—like you would scramble eggs before cooking an omelet.

In other words, without the helmet of salvation on, the devil will take all your thoughts, all the words that you have heard, and scramble them so that you will be confused. Once you scramble an egg, you can't separate it again—and that is kind of like what the devil tries to do. He knows that he cannot come in and just make you forget all that you have learned about Word of God. So, what he does is he tries to mix in some lies with the truth until, eventually, you're not sure if it's in the Bible or if someone like Confucius said it.

People get carried away if they are not careful, because something may sound good. Like cleanliness is next to godliness. That is not biblical. And as crazy as that sounds, the devil will build on that until he has you believing more lies and fables rather than the truth. That's why you hear people says things like, ""If it be the Lords will to heal me, then He will"." And they say that because they don't know enough of the word to keep them safe. The

Bible says in 1 Peter 2:24, "Our healing is a done deal, it is His will but unless you believe it you will not receive it."

The devil will come to you and tell you that you are not saved, that you are not a child of God. He will tell you that those words that you said are just words and they didn't change a thing—that God will not save someone like you. And that you have been too bad or that you have waited too long. Besides all of that, he will make you feel like you don't even feel saved.

Here is what the Bible says in Romans 10:9–10: "That if you confess with your mouth the Lord Jesus and believe in your heart that God raised Him from the dead, you will be saved. For with the heart one believes unto righteousness, and with the mouth confession is made unto salvation."

Glory to God, do you see that? Not one word about feeling saved was mentioned, was it? All you have to do is believe, and then 2 Corinthians 5:17 (NKJV) belongs unto you which says, "Therefore if anyone is in Christ, he is a new creation, old things have passed away; behold all things have become new."

There it is again. Nothing is mentioned about feeling. And if you think that sounds great, look at this: old things passed away; behold all things become new. Do you know what that is saying? It is saying that when you accept Jesus as Lord and savior of your life, God sees you as though you have never sinned.

Micah 7:18–19 (NKJV) says, "Who is a God like you, pardoning iniquity and passing over the transgression of the remnant of His heritage? He does not retain His anger forever, because He delights in mercy. He will again have compassion on us, and will subdue our iniquities. You will cast all our sins into the depths of the sea."

I know He is talking spiritual but He is relating it to something natural. And with that in mind, there are places so deep in the ocean man cannot go without dying. There are places so deep that it is said if a submarine was to go that deep, the pressure would crush it. And if that is not good enough, He said in Psalm 103:12 (NKJV), "As far as the east is from the west, so far has He removed our transgression from us."

There are astronomical objects that scientists have found that are 6,000 light years away. Now, a light year is the distance that light can travel in a year's time. Light moves at the speed of 186,000 miles per second. You do the math.

In other words, God will never remember your sins again. When He forgives, He forgets.

1 John 2:12 (NKJV) says, "I write to you little children, because your sins are forgiven you for His name sake. Once you repent and ask for forgiveness. God will not remember your sins no more. He has chosen to forget them."

Why am I telling you this? Because you may remember what you have done in the past. Your friends may remember what you have done in the past; your parents may remember what you have done in the past; your spouse may remember what you have done in the past; even your church may remember what you have done in the past—and I assure you the devil will remember what you have done in the past. He will bring it back to your remembrance. And when he does, if you have on the Helmet of Salvation, you can look at him and say, ""It may be true, but my Father has chosen to forget that and I do too. So, get behind me, Satan, for you are an offense unto me.""

I have been washed by the blood of the Lamb! I'm innocent!

You see, people have heard that God loves them and will forgive them or heal them or deliver them—but because they just heard it and never applied the Helmet of Salvation by studying the word for themselves, the devil comes and scrambles what they have heard and it gets them to believe a lie. If the devil can get you to believe a lie, then he's got you.

The helmet covers the mind, the head, and ears so the devil cannot mess with your mind. But you have to apply it every day by studying, praying and confessing who you are and what you have because of what Jesus did.

Understand that confusion is not of God. He has given us His word to study, and the Holy Ghost to teach us so that we won't be confused. So, when the devil comes to you and he brings up your past, and you remember what you did because we don't have the ability to just forget what we have done, remember we are saved. We can stand firm because, through studying the Word of God, we know that God has chosen to forget our past when we got saved.

The Roman soldier would not go anywhere without wearing his helmet. He could get stabbed with a knife and live—but if he got struck with a battle axe to the head, death was a sure thing. If the devil can get into your mind and confuse you, then he can destroy you and your walk with God. So, strengthen your helmet of salvation every day. Don't give the devil a chance to get into your thoughts.

We must wear our helmet so the devil cannot chop away at our minds and try to steal away our benefits of our salvation—and he will try. He will back away and tell you that you are a nobody, and that God does not really love you; and that your salvation is not real and that you cannot make it. That's why we must put on the Helmet of Salvation or else you will be vulnerable to the devils lies.

We must study our salvation and all that it includes. We have to know what Jesus' death and resurrection has purchased for us. Then it won't matter how hard the devil hits us with his lies because we will know Gods truth since we will have on the mind of Christ—we will have on our Helmet of Salvation.

CHAPTER EIGHT

The Sword of the Spirit

Ephesians 6:17 says, "And the sword of the spirit." (This is a power point. You have to take it!)

The sword that Paul was speaking about was a double-edged sword with the end turned upward. The purpose of this sword was to inflict maximum damage, more than any other sword made. Its purpose was to kill the enemy by ripping their insides to shreds. It only needed to penetrate the enemy two inches to mortally wound them. It was made to kill, to annihilate the problem.

Do you like it when your problem is annihilated? I am not talking about your problems easing up to the point to where you can live with them. I am talking about being annihilated to the point where they are no more; made to be non-existent. If so, I have good news.

Hebrews 4:12 (KJV) says, "For the Word of God is quick and powerful and sharper than any two edge sword piercing even to the dividing asunder of the soul and spirit and of the joints and marrow and is a discerner of the thoughts and intents of the heart."

So, the Word of God is our spiritual sword—but how do you use it? In Revelations1:6, the scripture tells us that it comes out of our mouth. You have got to open your mouth and speak the Word of God over your situations, in faith, if you ever want them to change.

In Matthew 4, the devil came and tempted Jesus by saying

1. ""turn these stones into bread.""
2. ""throw yourself off this temple"."
3. ""bow down and worship me"."

And what did Jesus do? He spoke the word *rhema*, the spoken Word of God.

1. ""man shall not live by bread alone but by every word that proceeds out of the mouth of God.""
2. ""You shall not tempt the Lord thy God"."

3. ""Thou shall worship only God and Him only shall you serve"."

Every time that Jesus spoke, His words where a spiritual sword that was thrust into His enemy. And in the end, His enemy left because he was defeated by the Word of God being used in faith.

People will tell you that they spoke the Word of God over the situation but nothing happened. That statement within itself is a statement of doubt because they have already given up, and now see it as a failed situation by saying that nothing happened.

When you start doubting, you start confessing the problem instead of the answer, the promises of the Word of God. You see, doubt looks at the situation while faith looks at the Word of God.

""I'm sick, but I am believing for my healing"" is a negative confession. And as long as that is your confession, you will never be healed because that is not faith speech.

Now, faith does not deny that there is a problem—it just denies the right for them to be there. Despite what I feel, despite what it looks like, I am healed! Your sickness may be fact, but faith in the Word of God spoken over that sickness will change it. Faith turns fact into truth.

Ephesians 5:1 (NKJV) says, "Therefore be imitators of God as dear children. In other words, be a shadow and copy how He acts and responds to a situation. Do what He does."

Well, what does He do? Romans 4:17 gives life to the dead and calls these things which do not exist as though they did. If you will speak faith over your situation and not doubt, you will never see it the same again because faith will see it fixed.

This is not positive thinking. I am not talking about mind over matter. This is called faith, and faith will speak that which the Word of God says.

The Bible says in Matt. 24:35, "Heaven and earth will pass away, but My words will never pass away." The Word of God is forever settled in heaven and always works if used in faith. The Word of God has got to be our foundation that we build everything upon. Psalm 119:89 says, "Your word is settled in heaven."

When a foundation is settled, that means it has quit moving, it is no longer changing. You cannot change the Word of God—God settled it, its unchangeable. But if you find your promises and confess them, and stand on the Word of God, He will make good on His word in your life and by faith the situations in your life will change.

Here is how important confession is. You can't even be saved unless you confess. Confess what? His promise of salvation by declaring or confessing Jesus as the Lord of your life.

Joshua 1:8 (KJV) says, "This book of the law shall not depart out of thy mouth but shalt meditate ther in day and night, that thou mayest observe to do according to all that is written there in, for then, after you have kept the word, meditated on it day and night, obeyed what the word says to do, then thou shalt make thy way prosperous and then thou shalt have good success, but first things first, the word has got to be in you."

This is the people's way: ""Give me success, then I will trust you"." This is God's way: ""Trust me then I will give you success."" Understand that Jesus was around thirty years old before He was tempted in the wilderness. And when the temptation came, He spoke rhema because He has already studied, meditated, and kept the Word of God.

So, when He spoke the Word of God, He was speaking it as truth no matter what it looked like. He knew the Word of God could not and would not fail. That's how He could heal the sick, open blind eyes, calm the wind and waves. He believed in the spoken Word of God.

I personally know people who say they have great faith—mountain moving faith. But when faced with adversities and trials, they crumble and give way to negative speaking. What happens in most cases is they know what the scripture says, but they don't have faith in what it says. They have a mental knowledge but not a spiritual knowing.

In some cases, they memorize scriptures just so they can look good. Here's a news flash: You cannot impress the devil enough for him to leave you alone. You must get the word inside of you and speak it out by faith.

Proverbs 6:2 tells us that, "You are snared by the words of your mouth." The word *snared* means overtaken. You are overtaken either by negative things or positive things. It all depends on which one you speak out of your mouth.

That is why Jesus was victorious. Philippians 2:7 (NKJV) says, "but made Himself of no reputation, taking the form of a bondservant and coming in the likeness of men." Jesus walked the earth as a man, not God. He left the trinity authority in heaven and walked in the authority that was given to mankind. 1 John 2:6 (NLT) says, "Those who say they live in God should live their lives as Jesus did."

Jesus said in John 4:12 (KJV), "Verily, verily, I say unto you, He that believeth on me (*are you a believer?*) the works that I do, shall he do also, and greater works than these shall he do because I go unto my Father."

Luke 10:19 (KJV) says, "Behold I give unto you power (*authority*) to tread on serpents and scorpions and over all the power of the enemy and nothing shall by any means hurt you."

The first word *power* in that verse is *exousia*, the executive power. It denies the rights of the presence of a hindrance. It says that, as a child of God, you have the right and the might to overcome your adversary!

The second word *power* is *dunimis*, destructive power or miraculous power—of what? Your enemy, your adversary, and, as 1 Peter 5:8 says that your adversary is the devil. So Jesus is telling us that we have the ability, the right, the means, or license—if you will—to be victorious over all opposition that we are faced with.

Mark 16:17–18 (KJV) says, "And these signs shall follow them that believes. In my name, they shall cast out devils, they shall speak with new tongues, they shall take up serpents, and if they drink any deadly thing, it shall not hurt them, and they shall lay hands on the sick and they shall recover."

Seven times in that verse, Jesus said that the signs will follow and be performed in the life of the believer. All of them. We don't pick and choose which ones we want. Jesus said all of them, for all believers. You could say that the sign are fruits of salvation. According to Jesus, if you're a believer, then you will have the signs.

Mark 11:23 (KJV) says, "For verily I say unto you, that whosoever (*anybody*) shall say unto this mountain, be thou removed and be cast into the sea and shall not doubt in his heart but shall believe that those things which he saith shall come to pass, He shall have whatsoever he saith."

So, what are you going to have? Whatever you say, because from the abundance of the heart the mouth speaks. You will speak what you really believe in the midst of those trying circumstances and situations that seem bleak—and whatever it is that you speak is what you're going to have.

People say all the time, ""That's not what I meant—I was frustrated or down and out at the time." But what is inside finds i's way out in these times. You see, it's a heart thing—not a mind thing. When you speak the Word of God from your heart in faith, there is a double-edged sword that flies out of your mouth and brings to pass that thing that you are believing. The key is, ""you have got to speak it by faith and not doubt"."

When you study and meditate on God's word, it will transform you. When you let the Word of God take root in your heart, it becomes part of your inner most being—not just merely words, but a part of you. God has given us His word, the Sword of the Spirit so that we can cut the devil and his schemes into pieces, and live a victorious life.

The sword is yours, it is up to you to use it. So, get the word into your heart then speak it out of your mouth. And when you do, the devil will flee, and situations will turn around for the good in your life.

CHAPTER NINE

Long Distance Prayer

Ephesians 6:18 says, "Praying always with all prayer and supplication in the spirit."

This is what I like to call the hidden piece of armor—the spear.

Roman soldiers' spears were made of wooded staffs with an iron spearhead. They would range anywhere from five to seven feet depending on the user. Roman soldiers were known to be highly skilled in the art of spear throwing. What is the art of spear throwing? What they would do is, as soon as the battle would first start, they would take off in full sprint and throw their spears at the oncoming enemy, wounding some—even killing some. The reason behind this strategy was when they got to the active battle, it was a lot easier to win because part of the enemy was already dead or wounded. So, all they would have to do to finish off the wounded was draw their sword and stab them, or stomp them with their hobnails.

Our long spear is praying in the spirit. It is a lot easier to battle something when it's a far distance from you, rather than when it's right in your face. Here's an example. If a bear was coming to attack you and he had his paws on you, that would be a rough situation to be in for you to come out victorious. But if he was hundred yards away and you had a rifle, then you would have a better chance of winning the battle. And that's how prayer works; it is our advantage.

We must realize that prayer is indispensable to us regardless of how skilled we think we are. We cannot maintain a life of victory apart from a life filled with prayer. You see, it is in prayer that you seek God's direction, His will, and His power for your life—and you need to do it on a daily basis.

Dick Eastman said, ""Prayer is the simplest act a creature of God can perform. It is divine communion with our Heavenly Father. Prayer is not a pre-requisite to engage in it. Only an act of the will is required to pray."

In Ephesians 6:18 (KJV), it says, "Praying always with all prayer and all supplication in the spirit."

The word *supplication* means to spend intimate time where we come before God in childlike faith, expressing our desires and ourselves whole enjoying His presence. You could say that supplication is freely enjoying fellowship in the presence of God, getting into an intimate setting—and it is in these times that we can use our spear, our long range spiritual weapon of prayer.

I want to talk about two different sizes of spears: the five-foot spear and the seven-foot spear. There are times that you know exactly what you need to pray about. Right after I got saved, I prayed against heart problems, diabetes, and cancer. You see, I attacked them before they could attack me. The five-foot spear was for shorter distance, so I relate it to the use of when a problem is coming, but it is not there yet—just like the heart problems, diabetes, and cancer. These are all hereditary diseases. I did not have any of them yet, but because of my family history, I could see them coming in the future since they ran in our family. Notice I said *ran*—past tense—because I stopped them from attacking me by using the short spear, the five-foot spear in faith.

You use the short spear when you know what is coming your way. How you use it is get the Word of God in your spirit, and use that word to pray against the attacks of the devil. Then believe that the problems are taken care of.

That is simple faith-prayer—ask, believe, and you shall receive. What are you going to receive? What you ask for and believe for. And I want to stress this: You have to ask in order to receive.

The Bible says in James 4:2, "You do not have because you do not ask." Jesus said in John 16:24 (NKJV), "Until now you have asked nothing in My name. Ask, and you will receive, that your joy may be full." Then in Matthew 7:7–8 (NKJV), it says, "Ask, and it will be given to you, seek, and you will find; knock, and it will be open to you. For everyone who asks receives, and he who seeks finds, and to him who knocks it will be open." And in Matthew 21:22 (NKJV), "And whatever things you ask, in prayer, believing, you will receive."

I hear people say, ""Well, God knows what I need, and if He wants me to have it, then He will give it to me." Not if you don't ask and believe for it. We are instructed in the word to ask for what we need, and in that, we need to realize that there is nothing too small or too big for God to do in the life of His child who asks in faith. So, begin to ask in faith so your joy may be full.

But what if you don't know what you need to pray for? But you just feel like you need to pray?

Romans 8:26–27 (NKJV) says, "Likewise the spirit also helps in our weaknesses. For we do not know what we should pray for as we ought (*and when that happens*) the spirit Himself makes intercession for us groanings which cannot be uttered."

Now, He who searches the hearts knows what the mind of the spirit is. Because He makes intercession for the saints, according to the will of God. And the will of God is His word.

The devil has plans against you, that you don't know about, to tear you down; to destroy your life. He wants to wreak havoc and cause you as much pain and destruction as possible. And that is why we need to pray in the spirit. The Holy Ghost knows the plans that are formed against you. And when you start praying in the Holy Ghost, there are spiritual long-range spears that leave your mouth and start attacking the plans that the devil has against you before he is able to manifest them in your life.

Praying in the Holy Ghost would be as what I relate to the Roman soldiers' seven-foot spear, and it is the best one because you use it before the enemy is even ready and fully-prepared to attack you.

The long spear is praying in the Holy Ghost, praying in tongues—so, in order to have this spear in your arsenal, you must be fully baptized in the Holy Ghost. There are different measures of operation of the Holy Ghost in a Christian life. The moment you get saved you have the Holy Ghost to a measure. You just don't have the fullness of Him unless the evidence of tongues is present.

Romans 8:9 (NKJV) says, "But you are not in the flesh, but in the spirit, if indeed the spirit of God dwells in you. Now if anyone does not have the spirit of Christ, He is not His."

1 John 5:7 (KJV) says, "For there are three that bear record in heaven, the Father, the Word, and the Holy Ghost, and these three are one."

There is only one spirit not four. There are different titles or names given to the Holy Ghost like The Spirit of Christ, The Spirit of God, The Holy Spirit, and the Holy Ghost. These are just different names given that describe the different aspects of who the Holy Ghost is. But there is only one Holy Ghost, and the moment you get saved, He moves into your heart. Understand, however, that you are not baptized or filled at that point.

In John 20:19–23, it says, "the disciples received the Holy Ghost but they were not baptized with the Holy Ghost until the day of Pentecost." The Bible says that He is my teacher, my comforter, my helper; not just for those who are baptized, but for all who are saved.

You see the word *baptized* means to be fully wet. The Bible calls it being filled. It is the fullness of the Holy Ghost and everyone needs to receive this measure. By going beyond the salvation measure and receiving the fullness of the baptism of the Holy Ghost, you receive the spiritual seven-foot spear, or praying in tongues.

Praying in tongues is the piece of the Armor of God that has been made available unto us to stop the problem before it can be completely formed. I am talking about the baptism of the Holy Ghost. It is more than goose bumps. It is more than just a tongue—the baptism in the Holy Ghost is a weapon! And to be fully arrayed in the Armor of God, you must be totally immersed in the Holy Ghost.

And just like all other parts of the Armor Of God, you need to apply and walk in its fullness every day.

Ephesians 5:18 (KJV) says, "and be not drunk with wine wherein is excess, but be filled with the spirit."

The Greek text makes it clear that it is not a onetime application. I prayed in tongues a year ago so I have it now. No! It is something that must be done over and over again. The Greek says being filled by something that is continual.

In the book of Acts, it says that the disciples were filled over and over again. In Acts 2:4 it says that they were filled with the Holy Ghost including Peter, and over in Acts 4:31 it also says that they were filled with the Holy Ghost.

The word filled in the Greek means to be wholly affected or influenced with or by something. The idea is like filling a sponge with water. It will hold the water for a while; but sooner or later, it will dry out again, and to be used, it needs to be wet again. As you scrub with it, the liquid leaks out. And when that happens, it is not as effective as it was when it was full. For it to be effective, it must stay wet until the job is done. To be effective we must stay filled until the job is done.

When was the last time that you were filled? Has it been awhile? Think about this question: How important is the baptism of the Holy Ghost? It is so important that Jesus commissioned the disciples, but before they could begin their ministry, Jesus said in Luke 24:49 (NKJV), "Behold I send the promise of my Father upon you; but tarry in the city of Jerusalem until you are endued with power from on high."

Why did He tell them to wait? Because Acts 1:8 says, "Ye shall receive power after the Holy Ghost is come upon you and you shall be witnesses unto me." That word *power* is *dunimis*—it is miraculous power and ability. It is divine power overcoming all resistance, just like dynamite. In other words, the baptism of the Holy Ghost brings power to overcome all attacks of the devil!

I dare you to shout, ""I have Holy Ghost Power"!" Do it again and again—that is building faith. Now, if you are not baptized yet but you want to be, the Bible says in Acts 1:4 to "wait for the promise of the father." Promise—the word tells what the promise of God is and then gives the assurance that the thing promised will be done.

And Acts 2:39 tells us that this promise of the baptism of the Holy Ghost is for everyone who will receive Him. It is about time that the body of Christ puts on the Armor of God and uses all the weapons that God has given to us to start tearing down the walls of hell, and making the devil give back what he has stolen from us.

It is time we stand up and tell the devil that we are here to take back our moms, our dads, our brothers, our sisters, our health, our wealth, and whatever else it is that he has stolen from us! And while you are at it, tell him that there is not anything that he can do about it because 1 John 4:4 (KJV) says, "Greater is He that is in you then he that is in the world." There is power and there is victory for the blood-bought child of God, and it is about time that you operate in it!

But to be truly, and completely armored up you must be baptized in the Holy Ghost with evidence of speaking in tongues. People received when Paul laid hands on them in Acts 19. Peter was preaching in Acts 10. The disciples were waiting and seeking in Acts 2. The point is that they received.

I ask you: Have you received the baptism of the Holy Ghost since you believed? If not, 'it's time!

ABOUT THE AUTHOR

Mark Fell has been in ministry for over 21 years and a senior pastor for over 12 years. He graduated from Rhema Correspondence Bible College. He is passionate about teaching Christians how to live a victorious life. He is married to his beautiful wife Angie and has two wonderful children, daughter Markeia and son Isaiah.

CPSIA information can be obtained
at www.ICGtesting.com
Printed in the USA
LVHW111321120620
657937LV00005B/1472